Partner With God

CONTENTS

PREFACE
BACKGROUND
ACKNOWLEDGEMENT

1. THE FOUNDATION
2. THE BUILDER
3. THE INSTRUCTIONS
4. THE TIMING
5. PLOWING/ BUILDING
6. WATCH & PRAY
7. CLOSURE

PREFACE

My name is Samuel Onumah, and I am a young man who feels immensely blessed that God chose me to be a vessel for writing this book. I am eager and grateful for the enrichment that it will bring to you. The inspiration for this book came to me during one night in the year 2022, while I was reading the book of Samuel. At that moment, I felt a profound sense of purpose and clarity that guided me through writing this book. This book will provide you with valuable insights and perspectives that will leave a lasting impact on your life.

While I was reading the book of Samuel, my aunty Felicia approached me and asked what I was reading. I responded to her "the book of Samuel," she smiled and said something that would change my life forever. She told me not to just read the book of Samuel, but to study the life of Samuel and pray that God would reveal my purpose to me, just as he did with the prophet Samuel. After that conversation, I started to dive deeper into the book of Samuel and began to seek God fervently. As time went on, I began to see myself transform into the likeness of Christ Jesus. I was no longer the same person who used to party, drink, smoke, and fornicate.

Now, I can proudly say I'm a new person in Christ Jesus. Samuel Onumah is a man who is after the heart of Abba Father. I am passionate about serving God and fulfilling the purpose that he has for my life. All thanks to my aunty Felicia's wise words and the guidance of the Holy Spirit.

As you take the time to delve into the pages of this book, my prayer is that you will experience a profound transformation that will leave an indelible mark on your life. This book intends to offer a personal message that will speak directly to your soul, challenge your thinking, and encourage you to align your heart with that of our Heavenly Father. The words within these pages are meant to inspire you to embrace a new perspective in Christ Jesus and approach this life with renewed vigor and purpose from him

Furthermore, you might feel convicted by the Holy Spirit while reading this book to confront areas of your life that may have been holding you back and encouraged to take bold steps toward the abundant life you were meant to live in Christ. I pray this book is a catalyst that propels you toward your destiny and the life that God has in store for you!

THE APOSTLE PAUL SAID, " I PLANTED THE SEED IN YOUR HEARTS, APOLLOS WATERED IT, BUT GOD MADE IT GROW."

➡ 1 CORINTHIANS 3:6

JOHN THE BAPTIST SPOKE THE FOLLOWING WORDS ABOUT JESUS: "HE MUST INCREASE, BUT I MUST DECREASE."
➡ JOHN 3:30

BACKGROUND

To provide a more comprehensive explanation of the notion of Partnering with God, I believe it is essential to elaborate on the triune nature of the Godhead, which comprises three distinct but inseparable divine persons, namely the Father, the Son (Jesus Christ), and the Holy Spirit. Which Partner With God is embedded in.

This concept of the Trinity asserts that the three persons of the Godhead are coequal, coeternal, and consubstantial, with each person possessing the fullness of the divine essence. By Partnering with God, individuals are invited to enter into a dynamic relationship with God, Holy Spirit and Christ.

As believers, we must be cognizant of the workings of the Holy Spirit in our lives, especially in these times. We need Him!

☆ ☆ ☆

There was a point in my life when I didn't pay much attention to my relationship with the Holy Spirit, until one day when the Lord spoke to me about the significance of his spirit. He made it clear to me that if I wanted to be considered a true son, I needed to be led by and work in partnership with his spirit. Additionally, he pointed out that many of the challenges, struggles, and disappointments I faced were a result of my failure to align myself with his spirit. The Holy Spirit is the key to unlocking our potential and fulfilling our divine purpose, and it is incumbent upon us to continually seek his guidance and direction in all aspects of our lives.

Our reliance on the Holy Spirit is paramount. Without his guidance, we may find ourselves disoriented, uncertain, or even led astray. The Holy Spirit is our compass, directing us toward the path of truth and righteousness. He is the beacon of light that illuminates the darkness of our doubts and fears, showing us the way forward. With him as our guide, we can traverse even the most treacherous terrain, confident in his wisdom and grace. This book that I have written would not have come to fruition without the unwavering support of our Heavenly Father and the constant guidance of his Spirit and strength. Throughout the process of writing, there were many days when I was overcome with emotion and found myself in tears, feeling as though I could not go on to writing the book due to weariness, warefare, e.t.c.

Despite these struggles, I knew that this was an assignment that had been ordained by God, and it was my duty to see it through to completion. There were moments when I felt the Holy Spirit speaking to me, urging me to move forward and offering me the strength and courage that I needed to keep going. Even when I had other plans or commitments, the Holy Spirit would disrupt my schedule, prompting me to focus on this project and reminding me that it was the will of the Father. Throughout the journey of writing this book, I learned to trust in God's plan and to rely on the Holy Spirit to guide my steps. It was a challenging and sometimes overwhelming experience, but I am grateful for the opportunity to have shared my story and to have fulfilled the purpose that God had for me by writing this book.

If you happen to be perusing through this book, you may be able to relate to the sense of wanting to engage in activities that you find enjoyable, such as watching a soccer game or participating in other leisurely pursuits besides praying or writing. However, there were instances where the Holy Spirit would bring to my attention the need to resist the temptation to give in to my fleshly desires. Instead, I was encouraged to devote my time to the secret place, where I could engage in a more spiritual and meaningful connection with God. This secret place could be a quiet room, a garden, or any other secluded area where I could meditate, pray, and reflect on my faith in a peaceful and reflective setting. It was in this secret place where I found the solace and strength to resist the lure of worldly distractions and focus on my spiritual growth, but better yet my development in God.

Throughout the accounts of numerous mothers who have been through the experience of pregnancy, it has become apparent that they often find themselves feeling irritated and overwhelmed by various things. Many of them even preferred to be alone during this time. Interestingly, I have also been strongly convicted by the Holy Spirit to pursue a similar feeling of being in isolation with the Father. This was to fulfill the important assignment that was given to me, and that was to write this book. It is only by being in a place of complete solitude and stillness, where one can connect with God on a deeper level, and truly embark on this journey with him and fulfill their purpose.

ACKNOWLEDGEMENT

I would like to express my sincere gratitude to all the leaders at the House of Destiny Door Global Ministries. I am incredibly grateful to Pastor Devin for his unwavering motivation, support, and guidance throughout my journey. His leadership has been instrumental in helping me grow spiritually and has enabled me to achieve my goals. I would also like to thank Pastor Gilbert Kiah and Apostle Jorah Kiah for their warm welcome and support. Their kindness and generosity have made me feel at home, and I am grateful for the opportunity to learn from them. They have played a significant role in shaping me into the man of God I am today, and I can't thank them enough.

Once again, thank you to all the leaders at House of Destiny Door Global Ministries. Your guidance and support have been invaluable, and I will always treasure the lessons I have learned from you.

☆ ☆ ☆

"Dear Prophet Ugo, I would like to express my heartfelt gratitude for the profound impact you have had on my life. Your teachings and guidance have been a great source of inspiration and motivation for me, and I am sure for many others in my generation. Your unwavering dedication and commitment to spreading the word of the Lord have been remarkable, and I feel blessed to have been touched by your divine influence. I am grateful for the way you have encouraged and challenged me to grow in my faith and to be a better person. Thank you for being a shining light in a world that desperately needs it.

I would like to express my deep appreciation and gratitude to my beloved mother, Grace Onumah, who has been my pillar of strength and biggest supporter throughout my life. Her unwavering love, guidance, and support have been instrumental in shaping me into the person I am today. From the very beginning, she has always been there, cheering me on and inspiring me to pursue my dreams, no matter how big or small. Her selflessness, kindness, and compassion are qualities that I truly admire and hope to emulate. I feel incredibly blessed and fortunate to have her as my mother, and I thank God every day for giving me such a wonderful gift. Mom, you are my hero and my role model, and I love you more than words can express. Thank you for everything!

1
THE FOUNDATION

Whatever we do in this life, a foundation has to be put in place and established before we can do anything that's to be sustainable, dependable, and reliable. Establishing a strong foundation is crucial in every aspect of our lives, whether it's our relationships, career, or any other venture. A solid foundation is the bedrock upon which we can build something that eternal. It lays the groundwork for our success by providing a stable and secure base that can withstand any challenges that come our way. With a not so solid foundation, the structure we build on top of it can be weak, and in the end eventually come crashing down. Therefore, it's essential to take the time to establish a firm foundation in God before we embark on any significant endeavor in life. By doing so, we can ensure that our efforts will be fruitful and that we can achieve our goals with confidence and ease in Christ.

In all aspects of life, the concept of a stable foundation is essential. Whether it is in constructing physical structures or building relationships, having a solid footing is key to ensuring long-lasting success. The creator of the heavens and the earth, our Father, understood this principle, and he made sure that we have an unbreakable foundation through the ultimate sacrifice of his son, our lord, and Savior Jesus Christ. The price that was paid for us to have this stable foundation is immeasurable and unparalleled, a testament to the tremendous love and compassion that our Father has for us. Through Jesus' sacrifice, we can have hope, peace, and security in our lives, knowing that we have a firm foundation to stand on. We can have confidence that our foundation is unshakable even in the midst of life's storms.

> *"PEACE I LEAVE WITH YOU, MY PEACE I GIVE TO YOU; NOT AS THE WORLD GIVES DO I GIVE TO YOU. LET NOT YOUR HEART BE TROUBLED, NEITHER LET IT BE AFRAID"*
> ➡ *JOHN 14:27*

Jesus' sacrifice not only provides a strong foundation for our individual lives, but it also forms the basis for our relationships with others. When we build relationships on the foundation of Christ's sacrifice, we can rest assured that they are built on a solid footing. Therefore, we should strive to build all our relationships on this stable foundation, trusting in the Lord's provision and guidance in all things.

As devout followers of the Christian faith, we are privileged to experience a distinct advantage in our daily lives through the unwavering foundation that Christ provides. His selfless act of sacrifice on the cross has left an indelible mark on humanity and serves as a guiding light for us as we navigate the complexities of life. By embracing this foundational pillar of faith, we can discover a sense of solace, purpose, and direction that empowers us to live our lives to the fullest. Every individual has a foundation upon which they build their belief system. This foundation can vary across different religions and cultures. For instance, Muslims consider Allah or Muhammed as the primary foundation for their beliefs, while Buddhists rely on the teachings of Buddha.

Similarly, other religions also have their unique foundations that they depend on to guide their principles, values, and practices. Despite the diversity in these beliefs, they all serve as a fundamental anchor for their respective followers, shaping their worldviews and guiding their actions.

☆ ☆ ☆

If you happen to be reading this book and you are feeling lost or uncertain about your foundation, I want to encourage you with the message that Jesus loves you deeply and desires to be the anchor in your life. His desire is for you to experience true freedom and to have a solid foundation built on him alone. My hope and prayer for you is that your heart would be softened by his love and that you would be led to a place of repentance and surrender.

It is no coincidence that you are reading this book at this moment; I believe that God has a specific purpose for you and wants you to know his love and grace more sincerely. May you be encouraged to seek him with all your heart and allow him to be the foundation upon which you build your life.

☆ ☆ ☆

As believers, we are constantly reminded that our spiritual foundation is of utmost importance. We are told that Christ should be the chief cornerstone upon which our faith is built. This means that we must continually strive to ensure that our faith rests solely on him. To achieve this, we need to dedicate ourselves to doing the necessary work that will enable Christ to be our foundation. We must make a conscious effort to abide in him, the Father, and the Holy Spirit every day. This involves reading His word, praying, and seeking his guidance in all that we do.

When we follow this command, we strengthen our foundation in Christ. We become more stable and firm in our faith. This stability allows us to weather the storms of life with greater ease, knowing that our faith rests on a solid foundation that cannot be shaken. Therefore, let us continue to build our faith on the firm foundation of Christ. As we do so, we can be assured that we will remain steadfast and immovable, no matter what challenges or trials we may face. Our relationship with Christ goes beyond just standing on him. But him desiring to dwell within us and for us to abide in him. This intimate connection with our Savior is what sustains us and gives us strength. As the psalmist wrote, when the foundation of our faith is shaken, we may wonder what the righteous can do. Let your foundation be Christ!

"IF THE FOUNDATIONS ARE DESTROYED, WHAT CAN THE RIGHTEOUS DO?
➡ PSALM 11:3

There is a crucial process that must take place in our lives after accepting Christ. This process involves examining and (DELIVERANCE), allowing God to uproot certain foundational belief systems that we held before fully surrendering to him. It's essential to recognize that some of these beliefs were due to our ignorance while we were still in the world, or they were passed down to us from our ancestors' generations. However, it's crucial to acknowledge that these beliefs are not the end of our journey. The good news is that the Holy Spirit is available to guide and lead us through this process of deliverance and transformation. With the help of the Holy Spirit, we can overcome these limiting beliefs and become all that God has called us to be.

I recently had a moment of deep reflection and self-realization. I concluded that a major reason for most of my struggles in life was mainly that I had not established a strong foundation in Christ before completely surrendering my life to Him. I realized that I was not deeply rooted in my faith and that it was hindering my spiritual growth and progress toward becoming a better person. As I delved deeper into my faith, seeking guidance, I was able to identify certain struggles that were not entirely my fault. I realized that some of these issues or problems were the result of ancestral agreements that my forefathers had made, which had been hindering my spiritual growth and progress without my knowledge. The Lord revealed this to me, and he is still revealing more to me.

This realization has empowered me to take steps toward strengthening my relationship with God and breaking free from the negative and evil patterns that have been holding me back. I am now more committed than ever to deepening my faith and living a life that is pleasing to God, and I am confident that he will continue to guide me on this journey with him. You must grasp the following statement, as it could lead to condemnation or feelings of guilt if left unaddressed. To uproot these erroneous foundations, a period of fasting and prayer is necessary. However, to ensure that you are targeting the core issue, it's crucial to conduct diligent research and seek divine guidance by asking the Father for wisdom and clarity. By taking these steps, you can confidently eliminate any false beliefs and move forward with a solid foundation.

> **"CALL TO ME, AND I WILL ANSWER YOU, AND SHOW YOU GREAT AND MIGHTY THINGS, WHICH YOU DO NOT KNOW.'**
> ➡ *JEREMIAH 33:3*

God, the father of all creation, deeply cares about our freedom. It is not his will for us to be in bondage, and that is why he sent his son, Jesus Christ, to deliver us from all forms of oppression. Jesus wants you to be completely in agreement with him and his kingdom of light, instead of being held captive by the forces of darkness. He desires to set you free from any chains that may be holding you back and to bring you into a place of true freedom and abundant life. So if you are struggling with any form of bondage or oppression today, know that Jesus is there to help you, and he wants nothing more than to see you free.

Prayer:

Father, please show me the roots of my problems in my life; you said in your word to call upon you, and you will show me a great and mighty things. For your plan is to prosper me and not to harm me. Where your spirit is, there is liberty, I believe that I am free in you. I come out of agreement with any thing that are not built on or from you. Let the precious blood of your son wash and cleanse me and my bloodline, let his blood speak for me, in Jesus' name I pray.

2
THE BUILDER

Being a builder for God; to be a builder for God, you have to be built up first. We are to trust God in this walk, but most importantly, to be effective builders for God, we must first ensure that we are being built up ourselves. We must cultivate a deep and abiding trust in God, recognizing that He alone is the source of our strength and wisdom. At the same time, we must also strive to earn God's trust by living our lives following his will and purposes. This involves seeking his guidance and direction, obeying his commands, and remaining faithful to him every moment of our lives. Ultimately, the key to being a successful builder for God is to focus on our relationship with him, trusting in his love and grace, and seeking to serve him with all our heart and soul.

We often overlook the importance of building ourselves up in the way that the Lord desires. It is crucial for us to constantly seek encounters with God and strive towards spiritual growth. By doing so, we can experience a transformative journey that leads us from one level of glory to the next. It is this continuous pursuit of Christ that helps us develop a deeper connection with our Abba Father and ultimately brings us closer to him. One of the most fulfilling experiences that we can have is being an honorable vessel before Him and the people around us. Our Heavenly Father understands the importance of living a life that reflects His values and principles, which is why he continuously works in our lives to mold us into the best versions of ourselves. This process can be compared to that of a builder who carefully constructs a building brick by brick, ensuring that every detail is just right. In the same way, God takes his time to shape us into honorable vessels, perfecting us day by day.

Despite our imperfections and shortcomings, our Father presents His mercy to us afresh every day, reminding us that his love for us is unconditional. We can always rely on him to guide us through life's challenges and to help us become the best versions of ourselves. So let us strive to honor him in all that we do, trusting that he will continue to work in us and through us for his glory. I've driven past beautiful architectural homes, and I told myself whoever put the design of this home together did a great job. Our Father God knowing a building is the work of the builder himself, and it represents him, rather if the building is good or bad. Our Father desires that man would look at us and glorify him. This means that every aspect of our lives should be in alignment with his will and purpose for us. If there are areas in your life that do not bring glory to God, I pray you would surrender it to him.

After all, God is the maker, potter, and creator of all things, which means that he knows what is best for us. By submitting to his plan and purpose, we can experience the fullness of life that he intends for us. I encourage you to seek God's guidance and surrender your life to him daily. It's important to address any unresolved issues that are brought to your attention, as ignoring them can lead to them resurfacing later on. The Apostle Paul recognized the importance of letting go of his own desires and ego to allow God's plan to unfold in his life, because of this we are able to read his epistles and relate resonate with them The more we yield to God, the more we will be able to see the full manifestation of his hand in our lives.

3
THE INSTRUCTIONS

Life is a journey that takes us through many twists and turns, and it can sometimes be hard to find our way. It is during these moments that we have to turn to our faith and seek guidance from God. He is a loving and caring Father who has a plan for every one of us, a plan that is intricately woven into the very fabric of our being. God's plan is not just a vague notion that we should follow. It is a detailed and specific roadmap designed to guide us through every step of our journey with him. His plan encompasses every stage of our lives, from infancy to old age, and everything in between. It is a plan filled with purpose, meaning, and direction.

However, when we stray from God's plan, it can cause him to be displeased. It's not that he is ashamed of us, but rather that he is disappointed that we are not living up to our full potential. God wants us to prosper and flourish in all aspects of our lives, not just in some areas. He desires to see us achieve our the dreams and aspirations he has crafted for us. In essence, God's plan is a blueprint for a life that is filled with joy, purpose, and fulfillment. It is a plan that is designed to help us live our best lives, to be the people/nation that we were meant and called to be. When we follow his plan, we can experience a life that is beyond our wildest dreams, one that is filled with blessings and abundance in and from him. God is not a source or author of confusion, but rather confusion arises when we get in the way of his plan.

When we experience confusion, we need to reflect and ask ourselves where it is coming from and what voice we are listening to. I felt a deep sense of urgency to pray for the Lord's bride and the burden that he carries for her. As a son of God, I have gained a better understanding of the chaos that his bride finds herself in at times due to her disobedience and pride. It is important for us, as the body of Christ, to remain humble before God daily, recognizing our need for guidance and help from him. Moses, before leading the people to inherit the land, recognized the importance of seeking God's guidance and help. We too must remain in a place of humility before God, seeking his guidance and direction in all that we do. It is only through our obedience to him that we can find true peace and clarity amidst the confusion that surrounds us.

"If your presence does not go with us, do not bring us up from here.
➡ *Exodus 33:15*

In life, we often have plans and goals that we want to achieve. However, it's important to ensure that these plans align with God's will for us. Sometimes, we may start building something that was never in God's plan for us, which can lead to our destiny he orchestrated being aborted or hindered. In Matthew 7 verse 24, Jesus emphasizes the importance of hearing and obeying His teachings. He compares those who do so to a wise man who builds his house on a rock. When the rain descends, the floods come, and the winds blow and beat against that house, it does not fall because it was founded on the rock. Likewise, when we build our lives on the solid foundation of God's word and follow his instructions for our lives, we can be assured that we are building towards a destiny that will not be aborted or hindered. Hearing and obeying God's word is a key to success in this life and also building a solid foundation.

Sometimes, our delays in life might not necessarily be the result of external factors or circumstances, but rather, our own disobedience. When we receive instructions from God, we must listen and submit to what he saying. If he tells us to take action, then we must act without hesitation. On the other hand, if he is asking us to wait patiently, then we must be patient and trust in his divine timing. As believers in Christ, we are called to be his disciples, which means that we have to be intentional about following him. To follow Christ means that we should always strive to be where he is and go where he goes. This requires us to be attuned to his voice, which we can do by spending time in prayer, reading and meditating on his word, and listening for the promptings of his Spirit. When we are sensitive to God's voice, we can be confident that we are moving in the direction that he wants to go.

To be a disciple of Christ is to follow him not just in word, but in action as well. This means that we must be willing to obey His commands and live according to his teachings and instructions. We must be ready to serve others and put their needs before our own. We should be quick to forgive and slow to judge, just as he was in the earth. By living in this way, we can be a light in the world and show others what it means to follow Christ. Ultimately, our goal as disciples of Christ is to fulfill the purpose that he has for our lives. We can do this by seeking his will in all things and trusting that he will guide us on the right path. When we walk in his footsteps, we can be confident that we are living a life that is pleasing to him and that will bring glory to his name.

"THE LORD DIRECTS THE STEPS OF THE GODLY. HE DELIGHTS IN EVERY DETAIL OF THEIR LIVES."
➡**Psalm 37: 23**

We must always be cautious and attentive as we seek to hear from God and receive his instruction. It's important to remember that the enemy also seeks to speak and guide us, so we must be mindful of his tactics. To guard against this, we must cultivate intimacy with the Father, Son (Jesus Christ), and Holy Spirit. When we know the voice of God, it becomes much more difficult for the enemy to lead us astray. Therefore, we must prioritize our relationship with God and learn to discern his voice above all others even our own. By doing so, we can confidently follow his guidance and avoid the pitfalls of the enemy's deception or going astray. The importance of reading and meditating on the word of God cannot be overstated. One of the reasons why it is essential is that it sharpens your discernment. This is because God will never go outside of his word; he is one with his word.

Furthermore, the enemy is always looking for ways to disrupt this process. He not only wants you to ignore God's word but also seeks to make you unstable, double-minded, and question God's goodness, just as he did with Adam and Eve. Therefore, you must be vigilant and guard your mind against his attacks. You should only have one mind, and that should be the mind of Christ. It's crucial to understand that the mind of the enemy is opposed to the mind of Christ. The mind is where insight and wisdom are stored, and it's from this place we make decisions. If you find yourself making poor decisions, it's worth examining what's stored up in your mind. Have your mind been filled with negative thoughts, lust, doubts, fears? or anything that is opposed to the mind of Christ. If so, it's time to replace them with the truth of God's word.

4
THE TIMING

The book of Ecclesiastes chapter 3 states that there is a time and a season for everything in life. It also highlights the importance of recognizing and understanding the timing and seasons that God has for our lives. The concept of time and season is profound, rooted in the very nature of creation itself. While we often think of time as a linear progression from past to present to future, time is much more fluid and complex than we can imagine. However, the enemy's goal is to distract us and cause us to miss these crucial seasons and divine timing God ordained for us. This is because the enemy operates in opposition to God's will, seeking to sow chaos and confusion wherever possible. It is up to us to be vigilant and stay in tune with God's plan for our lives so that we may walk in the fullness of his blessings and purpose.

God's timing is essential in everything that we do. As human beings, we often tend to get impatient and want things to happen according to our timeline. However, when it comes to doing business with the Lord, we must be willing to accept his timing. Many people make the mistake of going ahead of God, not waiting for his plan to unfold, or even giving up on Him altogether. It's important to understand that God's timing is always perfect. He knows exactly what we need when we need it, and how it should be delivered. Therefore, we must learn to trust in his timing, even when it doesn't align with our desires, expectations. By doing so, we can experience the fullness of his blessings and achieve the greater purpose he has for our lives. Trust is important in our relationship with God, and he does not offer us opportunities until we are prepared to receive them.

God is alpha and Omega; the beginning and the end of all things, the first and the last. This means that God is all-encompassing and complete. Moreover, the phrase "God will not give you an assignment that's not been finished" assures us that if God has given us a task, it can be accomplished. We can take comfort in knowing that God will equip us with all the resources and abilities needed to complete the task. With this assurance, we can move forward in confidence and faith, knowing that we can accomplish anything that God has set before us. Understanding that God does not require our help to accomplish his plans and purposes it's an important mindset to have. Instead, what God desires from us is our obedience and submission to his will.

This means that even when we don't understand what God is doing or why he is allowing certain things to happen in our lives, we can still trust in his goodness and wisdom. By choosing to submit to God's will and obey his commands, we can experience the peace and joy that come from knowing that we are in alignment with his purposes for our lives. It can be quite liberating to embrace the mindset that God does not depend on us. This perspective can serve as an effective defense mechanism against the onslaught of negative emotions such as anxiety, stress, worry, and fear that can often threaten to take hold of our present and future. By acknowledging that God's plans and purposes are not contingent on our abilities or shortcomings, we can free ourselves from the burden of feeling like we need to carry the weight of the world on our shoulders. This can be a powerful realization that shifts our focus away from ourselves and towards a greater sense of purpose and direction in Christ. Ultimately, the recognition that we are not indispensable to God's plans source of comfort, reassurance, and peace amid life's challenges and uncertainties. In times of frustration, it can be easy to feel overwhelmed and powerless. However, it is crucial to remember that God is unchanging and steadfast. Regardless of the season or circumstance, God remains constant and faithful. Therefore, we can have absolute confidence that whatever God chooses to do during that particular time will ultimately come to pass. This unwavering trust in God can provide peace and strength during difficult seasons. It is important to recognize that our current circumstances are only temporary, and God has a plan for our lives that we may not fully understand yet. By placing our faith in God, we can find solace in knowing that he is in control and will always remain by our side. This helps destroy the possibility of putting our trust in the outcome of the situation, rather than in God himself.

The Lord wants us to be excited about his move, but not to the point where it becomes our identity or our god. Throughout the history of Israel, the relationship between the people and God has been complex and fraught with challenges. One of the most persistent issues has been the impatience and stubbornness of the Israelites in their dealings with their divine Creator (God). They often demanded that God act on their timeline and in their preferred manner, and when their expectations were not met, they became rebellious and defiant. At times, this led them to turn away from the one true God altogether and seek refuge in false idols and other sources of comfort.

This pattern of behavior was particularly evident during periods of hardship and adversity when the Israelites felt abandoned by God and left to their own devices. In these moments of weakness, they succumbed to fear, doubt, and self-preservation, forgetting everything that God had done for them in the past. They failed to recognize that God's timing and methods are not always clear to us and that his plans for us are often far greater than we can imagine. Despite the Israelites' repeated disobedience and rebellion, God continued to extend his love and mercy towards them. He sent prophets to warn them of the dangers of their ways and to call them back to him. He performed miracles and wonders to demonstrate his power and faithfulness. And he ultimately sent his son to die for their sins and reconcile them to himself.

In the end, the story of Israel is a reminder of the importance of trust, patience, and humility in our relationship with God. It teaches us that we must be willing to submit to his will and timing, even when it is difficult or uncomfortable. And it shows us that God's love and faithfulness are unwavering, even in the face of our most stubborn and rebellious moments. When pursuing your assignment, it's essential to keep in mind that working closely with God is key to success. One thing to note is that staying as long as God wants you to stay in a season does not necessarily mean that you are on the wrong path or are not making progress. Instead, it could be an indication that there is still more to learn or that you are being prepared for what's next. Staying longer can help you gain a deeper understanding of yourself has his child and your purpose, as well as provide more clarity and direction. Therefore, it is vital to be patient and trust in his timing, as it may not always align with your own. By doing so, you can fulfill your calling.

5
PLOWING/BUILDING

This section highlights the importance of stewardship. Stewardship encompasses more than plowing; it demands taking full responsibility for the resources entrusted to one's care. One must diligently cultivate and nurture these resources, ensuring they flourish into a bountiful harvest with the assistance of the Holy Spirit. There is a page in this chapter that outlines potential barriers that may hinder us from fulfilling God's calling. As sons, and daughters its exremely crucial to trust in God's unique commandment for us, and do not let the traditions of Men hold us back from fulfilling our assignments. Please o not be swayed by the opinion of others who focus on superficial things such as cameras, lights, and the number of members. Instead, let your focus be on the presence of God in the ministry/assignment he has presented you.

Presently, in the church, if your ministry does not look like others' ministry then it must mean "God is not involved in that ministry or if the ministry does not appeal to the flesh then it's not worth following. When it comes to ministry, it should not be about the cameras, lights, amount of members there but about the dwelling of God. But it should be about Christ and his will!

The Pharisees and Sadducees encountered difficulty in following Christ's teachings and performing the Father's work due to their unfamiliarity with Christ's methodology. This, in turn, created a hindrance in their ability to assimilate and execute his instructions. In essence, the disparity between their accustomed ways and Christ's approach proved to be a formidable obstacle for the Pharisees and Sadducees, causing their inability to follow and implement his teachings effectively.

What causes believers to stop plowing	How to overcome
➡ Distractions	➡ Fasting
➡ Reverence for God	➡ Prayers
➡ Comparison	➡ Word of God
➡ Comfortability	➡ Worship
➡ Sin	➡ Faith in God
➡ Fear	
➡ Pride	
➡ Past	

What causes belivers to stop plowing	*How to overcome*

What causes believers to stop plowing	How to overcome

<u>This page and the next is left for you to write all the things in your life you can partner with God</u>

6
WATCH & PRAY

If you are planning to engage in any spiritual activity that involves building a connection with God, it is essential to be a person of prayer. Praying regularly and with sincerity enables us to communicate with God and seek his guidance and provision. A person of prayer is someone who devotes time every day to talking to God. Prayer helps us to develop a deeper understanding of our spiritual goals and align our actions with God's will. Therefore, if you want to build a strong relationship with God, it is crucial to make prayer a part of your daily routine. We need to consider prayers not merely as a request made to or from God, but rather as a fundamental commandment bestowed upon us by him. This means we should view prayer as a vital, non-negotiable, and serious aspect of our spiritual practice, a way to connect with Christ and align our lives to his will.

By seeing prayer as a commandment, we acknowledge our role as humble servants of God, recognizing that it is through our devotion, humility, and perseverance in prayer that we can receive his blessings, guidance, and protection. In essence, prayer becomes a way of life, a constant reminder of our dependence on God, and an expression of our love and gratitude, The act of prayer is commonly associated with a place of worship. Nonetheless, it is important to acknowledge the multifaceted nature of prayer, which becomes more profound as one matures and grows closer to God. At its core, prayer is a straightforward dialogue between God and his faithful children. As such, it is a vital means of communication through which believers can engage with Holy Spirit. It's crucial to understand the intricacies of prayer language, as it can vary depending on the assigment at stake.

Expanding your knowledge of prayer language can lead to a more meaningful relationship with God and increased effectiveness in your prayers. Let's take action and commit to growing in our prayer life so that we can become effective. We must bear in mind that if Jesus, the Son of God, made a habit of praying to the Father, then who are we to neglect prayer? Let us emulate his example and integrate prayer into our daily routine. Utilizing prayer, we can establish a line of communication with God and procure the resilience and direction we require to confront the difficulties that come our way. Prayer is where the transaction from heaven shifts to the heart of the vessel of God to influence and impact the Earth. The act of watching helps you to operate from your true position, which is seated with the Father in Heaven.

This position of authority gives you an upper hand over the kingdom of darkness. By watching, you can observe and discern the strategies of the enemy and take the necessary steps to counteract them. It is through prayer that you receive the guidance, strength, and wisdom that enable you to overcome any obstacle that comes your way.

CLOSURE

As you come to the end of this book, I hope that you feel not only fulfilled but also blessed by the message it contains. I pray that it has encouraged you to seek a deeper relationship with God and to partner with him in every aspect of your life. This is truly the best decision you can make. When you surrender your life to God, you are placing it in the hands of the one who knows you intimately and has a unique and special plan for your life.

Living for God alone may not always be easy, but it is worth it. When you choose to live a life that honors God, you will experience blessings beyond measure. God promises to honor those who honor him, and this is a promise that extends not only to you but also to your future generations.

Remember that God created you with a purpose and a plan. He knows every detail of your life, from the beginning to the end. So, seek him daily, and allow him to guide you through each stage of your life. As you do so, you will find that he reveals the path that he has set before you, and you will experience a joy and peace that can only be found in him.

Made in the USA
Middletown, DE
19 October 2024

62407458R10038